JUV/
QC
661
.F54
2002

ORIOLE

W9-CDO-188

R0402485030

waves : principles of light. electricity

Oriole Park Branch
Balmoral Ave.
cago, IL 60656

DISCARD

Waves

Principles of Light, Electricity, and Magnetism

Secrets of the Universe

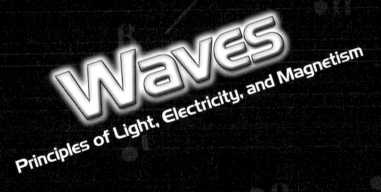

Waves
Principles of Light, Electricity, and Magnetism

by Paul Fleisher

Lerner Publications Company · Minneapolis

For Vanessa

Copyright © 2002 by Paul Fleisher

All rights reserved. International copyright secured. No part of this book may be reproduced, stored in a retrieval system, or transmitted in any form or by any means—electronic, mechanical, photocopying, recording, or otherwise—without the prior written permission of Lerner Publications Company, except for the inclusion of brief quotations in an acknowledged review.

The text for this book has been adapted from a single-volume work entitled *Secrets of the Universe: Discovering the Universal Laws of Science,* by Paul Fleisher, originally published by Atheneum in 1987. Illustrations by Tim Seeley were commissioned by Lerner Publications Company. New back matter was developed by Lerner Publications Company.

Lerner Publications Company
A division of Lerner Publishing Group
241 First Avenue North
Minneapolis, MN 55401 U.S.A.

Website address: www.lernerbooks.com

Library of Congress Cataloging-in-Publication Data

Fleisher, Paul.
  Waves : principles of light, electricity, and magnetism / by Paul Fleisher
      p.   cm. — (Secrets of the universe)
  Includes bibliographical references and index.
      ISBN 0-8225-2987-4 (lib. bdg. : alk. paper)
    1. Electromagnetic waves—Juvenile literature. [1. Light. 2. Electricity.
  3. Magnetism.] I. Title. II. Series. Fleisher, Paul. Secrets of the Universe
  QC661.F54 2002
  539.2—dc21   00-012120

Manufactured in the United States of America
2 3 4 5 6 7 – JR – 08 07 06 05 04 03

R0402485030

Contents

ark Branch
. Balmoral Ave.
Chicago, IL 60656

INTRODUCTION

Everyone knows what a law is. It's a rule that tells people what they must or must not do. Laws tell us that we shouldn't drive faster than the legal speed limit, that we must not take someone else's property, that we must pay taxes on our income each year.

Where do these laws come from? In the United States and other democratic countries, laws are created by elected representatives. These men and women discuss which ideas they think would be fair and useful. Then they vote to decide which ones will actually become laws.

But there is another kind of law, a scientific law. For example, you'll read about Coulomb's law later in this book. Coulomb's law tells us that the electrical force between any two objects depends on two things: the amount of electrical charge of each object, and the distance between the objects. Where did Coulomb's law come from, and what could we do if we decided to change it?

Coulomb's law is very different from a speed limit or a law that says you must pay your taxes. Speed limits are different in different places. On many interstate highways, drivers can travel 105 kilometers (65 miles) per hour. On crowded city streets, they must drive more slowly. But electrical force works exactly the same way no matter where you are—in the country or the city, in France, Brazil, or the United States.

Sometimes people break laws. When the speed limit is 89 kph (55 mph), people often drive 97 kph (60 mph) or even faster. But what happens if you try to break Coulomb's law? You can't. If you test one thousand electrically charged objects, you'll find that each and every one follows the rule described in Coulomb's law. All objects obey this law. And we know that the law stays in effect whether people are watching or not.

Coulomb's law is a natural law, or a rule of nature. Scientists and philosophers have studied events in our world for a long time. They have made careful observations and done many experiments. And they have found that certain events happen over and over again in a regular, predictable way. You have probably noticed some of these patterns in our world yourself.

A scientific law is a statement that explains how things work in the universe. It describes the way things are, not the way we want them to be. That means a scientific law is not something that can be changed whenever we choose. We can change the speed limit or the tax rate if we think they're too high or too low. But no matter how much we might want electrical forces to work differently, Coulomb's law remains in effect. We cannot change it; we can only describe what happens. A scientist's job is to describe the laws of nature as accurately and exactly as possible.

The laws you will read about in this book are universal laws. That means they are true not only here on Earth, but elsewhere throughout the universe too. The universe includes everything we know to exist: our planet, our solar system, our galaxy, all the other billions of stars and galaxies, and all the vast empty space in between. All the evidence that scientists have gathered about the other planets and stars in our universe tells us that the scientific laws that apply here on Earth also apply everywhere else.

In the history of science, some laws have been found through the brilliant discoveries of a single person. But ordinarily, scientific laws are discovered through the efforts of many scientists, each one building on what others have done earlier. When one scientist—like Charles-Augustin de Coulomb—receives credit for discovering a law, it's important to remember that many other people also contributed to that discovery. Almost every scientific discovery is based on problems and questions studied by many earlier scientists.

Scientific laws do change, on rare occasions. They don't change because we tell the universe to behave differently. Scientific laws change only if we have new information or more accurate observations. The law changes when scientists make new discoveries that show the old law doesn't describe the universe as well as it should. Whenever scientists agree to a change in the laws of nature, the new law describes events more completely or more simply and clearly.

A good example of this is the laws that describe electricity and magnetism. Scientists once thought that electricity and magnetism were two separate and different things. But new discoveries and improved measurements helped a great scientist, James Clerk Maxwell, rewrite the laws that describe how electricity and magnetism work. Maxwell realized that electricity and magnetism are two different forms of the same force. You will read about Maxwell's discoveries later in this book.

Natural laws are often written in the language of

mathematics. This allows scientists to be more exact in their descriptions of how things work. For example, Coulomb's law is actually written like this:

$$F = K \times \frac{q(1) \times q(2)}{d^2}$$

Don't let the math fool you. It's the same law that describes how electrical charges interact. Writing it this way lets scientists accurately compute the actual electrical force in many different situations here on Earth and elsewhere in the universe.

The science of matter and energy and how they behave is called physics. In the hundreds of years that physicists have been studying our universe, they have discovered many natural laws. In this book, you'll read about several of these great discoveries. There will be some simple experiments you can do to see the laws in action. Read on and share the fascinating stories of the laws that reveal the secrets of our universe.

CHAPTER 1

When we look into the sky at night, we see the light from thousands of different stars. We see the Moon and the planets, shining with reflected sunlight. The whole universe sparkles with light. But what is light, and what natural laws describe its behavior?

The branch of physics that studies light is called optics. Some of the world's greatest scientists, including Newton, Huygens, Maxwell, and Einstein, have studied optics, trying to understand the laws of light.

One law that describes the behavior of light has been known for two thousand years. The Greek philosophers didn't know what light was, but they did know that it travels in straight lines. The *law of reflection* depends on this fact. When light bounces off a mirror or other surface, this is known as reflection. When you see yourself in a mirror, you are seeing light that has reflected from your face to the mirror and then back to your eyes. The law of reflection says: The angle of incidence is equal to the angle of reflection.

The angle of incidence is the angle of the light shining onto the reflector. The angle of reflection is the angle of the light bouncing off the reflector. The law of reflection says that those two angles are always equal. If a light shines on a mirror at a 45-degree angle, it will bounce off the mirror at that same angle. The same is true no matter at what angle the light is shining.

You can easily see the effects of this law by using a small mirror, a flashlight, some cardboard and tape, and a little bit of chalk dust or flour. Draw a straight line down the center of a square piece of cardboard. Then fold the cardboard in half along this line. On a second piece of cardboard, trace

You can see the path of light reflections by shaking fine powder into the air.

around the lens end of your flashlight. Cut along your traced line, then poke a small hole in the center of the cut-out shape. Cover the lens of the flashlight with it, taping it securely in place. That will give you a narrow beam of light when you turn on the flashlight.

Place the mirror on a table. Stand the folded piece of cardboard on the table, centered behind the mirror. This will give you a vertical line to use to compare the angles of the light beam. Shake a very small amount of the chalk dust or flour into the air, to make the beam of the flashlight visible. Darken the room and shine the light onto the center of the mirror.

Notice that the beam of light bounces off the mirror at the same angle that it hits the mirror. It doesn't matter at what angle you hold the flashlight beam. The angle of the light reflected from the mirror will always match it exactly.

Light travels in straight lines. But light also bends when it travels from one kind of transparent material to another. If you stick a pencil into a glass of water, the pencil will appear to bend where it enters the water.

Of course, the pencil doesn't actually bend. It looks bent because the light traveling through the water bends. This bending of light is called refraction. Notice that the pencil seems to bend only at the surface of the water, where the water and air meet. Refraction takes place only at the boundary between two transparent materials.

Each transparent substance bends light at certain predictable angles. Refraction occurs because light travels at different speeds in different substances. The amount of refraction depends on the difference in the speed of light in the two transparent materials. The bigger the difference in the speed of light between the two materials, the more the light will bend as it passes between them.

Light travels faster in air than it does in water. When light moves from air to water, it slows down. And as it does, it also refracts, or bends. Light travels even more slowly in glass. When light moves from air to glass, it bends even more. A pencil placed partly behind a thick piece of glass would seem to bend even more than the pencil in water.

One scientist who studied optics was Isaac Newton. Newton knew that when sunlight is refracted in a glass prism, the white light breaks up into a rainbow of colors, called a spectrum. Newton proved that sunlight is actually composed of all the colors of the rainbow.

Many years later, the astronomer William Herschel discovered the existence of another kind of light—light that can't be seen. In 1800 Herschel was measuring the temperature of the different colors in the spectrum. He wanted to find out whether red, orange, yellow, green, or blue light produced the most heat. He used a glass prism to break sunlight into a spectrum. Then he measured each of the colors with a thermometer.

A surprising rise in temperature led Herschel to discover the existence of invisible infrared light.

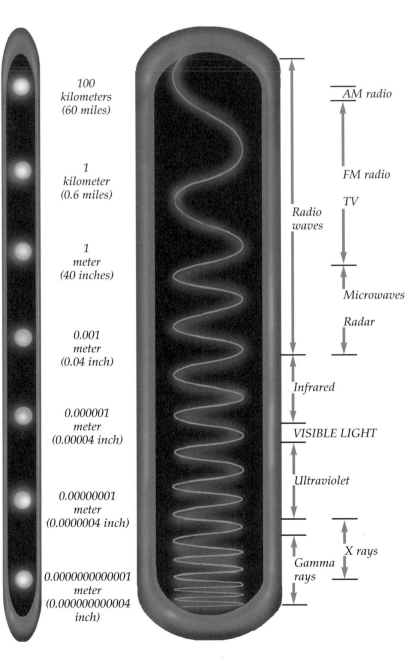

100
kilometers
(60 miles)

1
kilometer
(0.6 miles)

1
meter
(40 inches)

0.001
meter
(0.04 inch)

0.000001
meter
(0.00004 inch)

0.00000001
meter
(0.0000004 inch)

0.0000000000001
meter
(0.000000000004
inch)

AM radio

FM radio

TV

Radio
waves

Microwaves

Radar

Infrared

VISIBLE LIGHT

Ultraviolet

X rays

Gamma
rays

The electromagnetic spectrum includes an extremely wide range
of light waves.

Herschel found that the hottest part of the spectrum was alongside the red part, in a place where he couldn't see any light at all! But the thermometer proved that some invisible light rays were there. Herschel had discovered the existence of infrared light.

One year later, light on the other side of the visible spectrum was found. This light couldn't be seen either, but it did form images on photographic plates. This light became known as ultraviolet light. In the mid-1800s, James Clerk Maxwell showed that the spectrum of light includes much more than just the light we can see. We now know that the entire spectrum includes not just visible light, but also radio waves, infrared light, ultraviolet light, X rays, and gamma rays.

Newton's studies of light in the late 1600s and early 1700s started one of the longest debates in the history of science. The debate, which wasn't settled for more than two hundred years, was over the question of whether light is a shower of tiny particles or a series of waves.

To understand the question, you need to know something about the behavior of waves. Waves can be seen most easily in a wave tank. To make a wave tank at home, you'll need a clear glass baking dish, a sheet of white paper, and a bright desk lamp. You will also need two pencils and several small blocks of wood to make obstacles for the waves.

Fill the baking dish about two-thirds full of water. Place it on a table, on top of the sheet of paper. Place the lamp so that it shines down on the water from directly above. Now tap the water in the pan with the eraser end of a pencil to create some waves. You'll see that the waves create shadows on the paper below, making them easier to see. Remember that the waves you are seeing are water waves, but other waves, including light, have similar properties.

Place a small wooden block in the pan as an obstacle. On one side of the block, make some waves with your pencil. Watch what happens when the waves go past the obstacle.

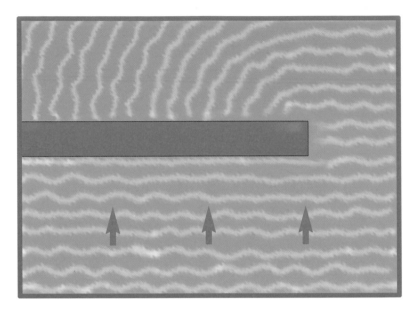

In a wave tank, waves diffract, or curve, around an object placed in their path.

Notice that the waves curve around the obstacle and travel into the part of the tank that is blocked off. This curving of waves around an obstacle is called diffraction. Diffraction is a characteristic of all waves.

To scientists in the 1600s, light didn't seem to diffract the way other waves do. Light seems to travel in straight lines, instead of curving around obstacles. If you place an object in sunlight, it casts a shadow. If light diffracted as water waves do, you would expect the light to bend around the object and make a fuzzy shadow. But light casts a shadow with sharp edges.

Because of this, Newton believed that light must be made of many tiny, swift particles moving in straight paths. When an object interrupts the particles, sharp-edged shadows are the result.

After Newton suggested that light is made of particles, two other noted scientists disagreed. Robert Hooke and

If light were made of particles, you would expect sharp shadows *(top)*. If light were made of waves, you would expect the shadow to be less distinct *(bottom)*.

Christiaan Huygens pointed out that light also behaves like waves. Let's use the wave tank again to show their side of the argument.

Block off one section in your wave tank, leaving only a small central opening to the rest of the tank. With your pencil, make some waves in the blocked section of the tank. Notice what happens when they pass through the opening.

The waves coming through the opening spread out just the way they spread out from the source of the waves itself. Huygens noted that any point along a wave can act as if it is a new source of more waves. The waves from this new source will have the same characteristics as the original waves. This rule is known as *Huygens' principle.*

That's exactly what happens when you allow light to shine through a small hole. It spreads out from the opening, just as if that opening were the source of the light.

Huygens also pointed out that if light were made of waves, that would explain its property of refraction. Light waves moving through different materials would travel at

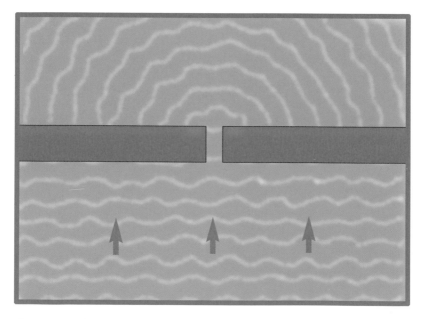

In a wave tank, waves passing through a small opening spread out just as if the opening were the actual source of the waves.

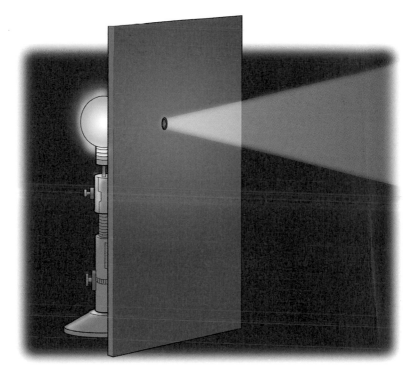

Light passing through a small opening behaves as if the opening itself were the light source.

different speeds. The change of speed would cause the waves to bend. It was harder to explain why "particles" of light should bend as they pass into water or glass.

Waves have another interesting behavior that is called interference. To see interference in your wave tank, you will need to make waves with two pencils. Hold the pencils a couple of inches apart. Then tap the surface of the water with both of them at the same time, in a regular pattern, creating two sets of waves.

Notice that as the two sets of waves overlap and cross, they interact with each other. In some places they cancel each other out, and in other places they add to each other's effects. This is called interference. If you keep up a steady

Two wave sources produce a pattern of interference.

pattern of waves with regular movements of your pencils, you should get a steady pattern of interference.

It's a characteristic of waves that they produce interference patterns as they cross each other. When streams of particles cross, we would expect them to collide. No one has observed collisions when two beams of light shine across each other. But does light produce interference?

In 1801 the English physicist Thomas Young proved that light does diffract and does produce interference patterns, just as other waves do. It seemed that the light/particle question was finally resolved.

You can easily see an interference pattern of light using two pencils and your desk lamp. Hold the two pencils in front of your eye as you look toward the lamp. Move the pencils closer together, until they are almost touching. You will see a pattern of very fine light and dark lines. That is the interference pattern produced as light from the lamp passes through the narrow slit between the two pencils. The dark lines are the places where the waves of light are canceling each other out. Since light produces interference patterns as other waves do, it too must be a wave.

Young also calculated the actual size of light waves. The wavelengths of light waves are very small, but Young managed to measure them. Different colors of light turned out to have different wavelengths. Young found that the wavelength of red light is about 76 millionths of a centimeter (30 millionths of an inch). The wavelength of blue light is even smaller, about 38 millionths of a centimeter (15 millionths of an inch).

Young's measurements explained why the diffraction of light is so hard to see. Diffraction occurs when waves bend around an obstacle. But light waves are so tiny that they can bend only around tiny obstacles—obstacles not much bigger than the size of atoms.

By the mid-1800s, it seemed certain that light was made of waves. But even then the question wasn't settled. Around 1900 new discoveries by Max Planck and Albert Einstein brought back the particle theory. The end result turned out to be that both sides of the debate were right! Light usually behaves like a wave, but it acts like a particle too.

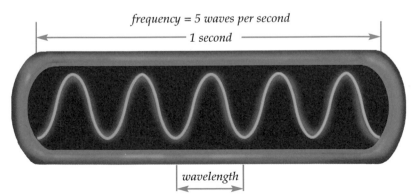

frequency = 5 waves per second

1 second

wavelength

Waves can be measured by their wavelength or by their frequency.

Is there a law that describes the brightness of light? Yes. The faint stars that we see in the night sky are actually blazing suns. Their light is much dimmer after its long journey to our planet. The farther you get from a light source, the less bright the light appears. In fact, the intensity of light from any source decreases very rapidly as the distance from the source increases. The decrease is proportional to the square of the distance. Squaring the distance means multiplying the distance times itself.

This special relationship between brightness and the distance from the light source is called an inverse square relationship. Many other forces in nature weaken with distance in similar ways. A more detailed explanation of why this is so begins on page 44. In the meantime, just think how much light our Sun must produce. It is extremely bright, even though we are about 150 million kilometers (93 million miles) away!

We need to consider one more fact about light—its speed. Galileo Galilei was the first scientist to try measuring the speed of light. He stood on a hill with a covered lantern and placed an assistant on a distant hill with a second lantern. He uncovered his lantern. As soon as his assistant saw the light, he was supposed to uncover his lantern. Galileo planned to measure the time it took for him to receive the signal back again.

Unfortunately, the experiment didn't work. The light seemed to travel between the two hilltops almost instantaneously. Light moves so fast that measuring its speed is very difficult.

The first successful attempt to measure the speed of light used Earth's orbit as a measuring stick. The Danish astronomer Olaus Rømer knew when eclipses of Jupiter's moons were scheduled to occur in the late 1600s. He noticed that the timing of the eclipses varied, depending on where Jupiter and Earth were in their orbits. If the two planets were on opposite sides of the Sun, the eclipses were a few minutes late. If the two planets were on the same side of the Sun, the eclipses were a few minutes early.

Rømer realized that the time difference was caused by the difference in distance that the light from Jupiter's moon had to travel before it was seen on Earth. Rømer knew the approximate diameter of Earth's orbit. He knew how much extra distance the light had to travel to cross that orbit. So he could estimate how fast the light traveled to cross that distance. Rømer calculated that light travels at about 226,000 kilometers (140,000 miles) per second.

In 1849 the French physicist Armand Fizeau was the first scientist to create a device to measure the speed of light in a laboratory experiment. Since that time, many other researchers have made more and more exact measurements of the speed of light. The most famous of them was the

Rømer used different positions of Earth's orbit to measure the speed of sunlight reflected from Jupiter.

American physicist Albert Michelson. He devoted most of his life to accurately determining the speed of light. Michelson won the Nobel Prize in 1907, in honor of the many ingenious experiments he used to measure the speed of light as precisely as possible.

Scientists now put the speed of light at 299,792.5 kilometers per second, or 186,281.7 miles per second. Those speeds are usually rounded off to 300,000 kilometers per second, or 186,000 miles per second. This is a very important measurement. The speed of light can be considered the "speed limit" of the universe. As far as we know, it is impossible for anything to travel faster than the speed of light.

The speed of light is 300,000 kilometers per second in a vacuum (totally empty space). Light travels almost as fast in air. In other materials, such as water or glass, the speed of light is much slower. For example, light travels about 225,000 kilometers per second (140,000 miles per second) in water and about 200,000 kilometers per second (124,000 miles per second) in glass. It is this difference in speed that causes light to refract, or bend, when it moves between one substance and another.

Light is such a familiar part of our everyday world that it's easy to forget how special and important it is. We can see our world only because it is bathed in a constant stream of light, which reflects off of the objects around us and into our eyes. The universe is full of light traveling at enormous speeds from distant stars and galaxies. It is this light that lets us know what's "out there" beyond our own world. Light is our most important connection to everything in the universe that lies beyond our own planet. Without an understanding of light, science could never understand the rest of the universe at all.

CHAPTER 2

Laws of Electromagnetism

In the late 1700s, electricity was a popular amusement at parties. Guests would collect electrical charges using glass rods and scraps of silk. Then they would shock each other with electric sparks, making their hair stand on end, and do other electrical parlor tricks. Electricity was a fascinating toy. But it also was a puzzle to the scientists who were trying to study it.

The most popular theory of electricity at that time said that electricity was made of two fluids. One fluid had a positive charge, and one was negative. There were many ways of collecting these fluids. For example, rubbing a glass rod with fur transferred some of the fluids, creating an electrical charge. The opposite fluids would then attract each other. But no one had seen electrical fluids or found any other evidence that they really existed.

No single scientist was responsible for discovering all principles that describe electrical forces. James Clerk

Maxwell was the scientist who finally wrote the complete set of laws for the workings of electricity and magnetism. But the mathematical laws that Maxwell published in 1864 were the result of many years of work by many different scientists.

Let's begin the story with Benjamin Franklin. You probably know that Franklin was a great American statesman, writer, and inventor. But he was also an early investigator of electricity. Franklin realized that electricity could be explained just as easily with one fluid as with two. Positive charge could be considered to be an extra amount of the fluid. Negative charge would then be a shortage of the same substance. The fluid theory didn't last, but Franklin's idea of positive and negative charges being two sides of a single force did.

Franklin also recognized a very important law of electricity: the *law of conservation of charge.* The law of conservation of charge says that for every negative charge created, there must be an equal amount of positive charge. That means that the total of all positive and negative charges in the universe must balance each other perfectly.

The law of conservation of charge doesn't mean that we can't have any electricity. But whenever we unbalance electrical forces, we must create positive and negative charges in equal amounts. For example, you can create an electrical charge by rubbing an inflated balloon against a wool sweater. The balloon will pick up a slight negative charge from the wool. But the wool will also receive an equal amount of positive charge. The balloon will then stick to a wall because of the difference in electrical charge between the wall and the balloon.

The same thing happens when we shuffle our feet across a rug on a dry day. As we walk across the rug, our body picks up a small electrical charge. An equal amount of opposite charge is built up in the rug. When you touch a doorknob or other metal object, the charges cancel out with a tiny spark. If you do this in a dark room, you will be able to see the spark clearly.

It's important to remember that whenever we give one object a negative charge, we give the other object a positive charge at the same time. The wool gets just as much positive charge as the balloon gets negative charge. Each object receives a charge, and the charges balance each other. That is the law of conservation of charge.

The next discovery of electrical law was made by the French scientist Charles-Augustin de Coulomb in 1789. Coulomb knew that opposite electrical forces attract each other and that like forces repel each other. He wanted to measure the strength of that attraction.

To measure electrical force, Coulomb suspended a rod from a thin wire. (See the diagram on the next page.) At each end of the rod was an electrically charged ball made of a corklike material. He then gave an opposite charge to two other balls nearby. He knew exactly how much charge each ball had. By measuring the amount of twist in the wire, he was able to calculate the force of attraction between the balls.

Coulomb's results were surprising and exciting. He discovered that electrical force is directly proportional to the amount of charge in the two objects and inversely proportional to the square of their distance.

Before we go on, it's important to understand what directly proportional and inversely proportional mean. They are not as difficult as they may sound.

If two measurements are directly proportional, when one increases, the other increases too. For example, if you are driving at 80 kilometers (50 miles) per hour, the distance you cover is directly proportional to the amount of time you drive. As time increases, so does distance. The longer you drive, the farther you go.

If two measurements are inversely proportional, then as one increases, the other decreases. For example, if you are

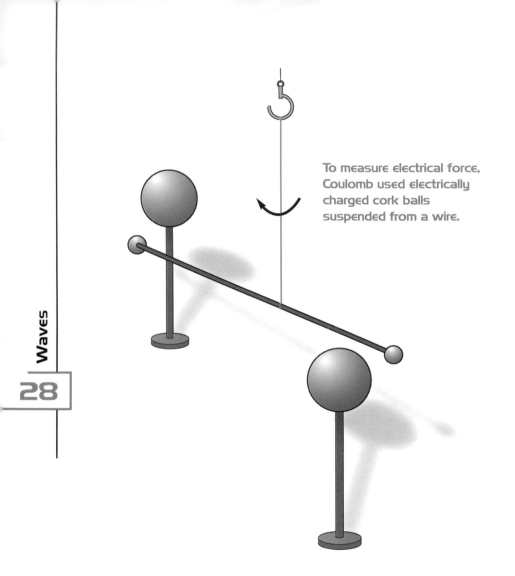

To measure electrical force, Coulomb used electrically charged cork balls suspended from a wire.

taking a trip of 160 kilometers (100 miles), the time of the trip will be inversely proportional to the speed that you drive. The faster you drive, the shorter the time of the trip. As the speed increases, the time decreases.

   Coulomb's law tells us that the electrical force between two charges depends on the strength of the two charges. The larger the difference in the electrical charges between two objects, the stronger the attraction between them. It also means that as two objects get farther apart, the attraction decreases rapidly. If two objects are moved twice as far apart, the attraction is only one-fourth as much. If they are moved three times as far apart, the force is only one-ninth as much.

Mathematically, Coulomb's law is written like this:

$$F = K \times \frac{q(1) \times q(2)}{d^2}$$

In this equation, F stands for the force of attraction, $q(1)$ and $q(2)$ are the charges of the two objects, and d represents the distance between the objects. K is a constant, a small number that allows the amount of attraction to be calculated precisely.

Coulomb also experimented with magnetic force in the same way. It turned out that the law of magnetic attraction was also an inverse square law. It was very exciting to discover that these different forces follow similar laws. It showed that the laws of the universe must fit into a simple and orderly pattern.

The next important discovery about electricity was made by Hans Christian Ørsted in 1820. Ørsted made his discovery by accident. He connected a wire to a battery to make an electric circuit. A magnetic compass happened to be sitting on the laboratory table nearby. Ørsted noticed that when electricity was flowing through the wire, the compass needle was attracted to it.

After more experimenting, Ørsted was sure of his discovery: A moving electrical charge creates magnetic force. Whenever an electric current flows through a wire, it creates magnetic forces around the wire.

You can do Ørsted's experiment yourself. All you will need is a length of insulated wire, a small magnetic compass, and a battery. Use a 1.5-volt dry cell or a 6-volt flashlight battery.

An electric current flowing through a wire creates magnetic force, as this simple experiment shows.

Strip a small amount of insulation off each end of the wire. Attach one end of the wire to one terminal of the battery. Form the wire into a loop and place the compass near the loop of wire. Arrange the wire in such a way that the compass needle is not pointing directly toward the wire. Now touch the free end of the wire to the other pole of the battery. Watch how the compass responds. Try the experiment with the compass and wire in several different positions. Don't leave the wire connected to both poles of the battery for more than a few seconds at a time. If you do, the completed circuit will quickly drain the energy out of the battery and the wire could become dangerously hot.

After 1820 the study of electricity and magnetism moved at a very rapid rate. Ørsted had found that electricity could exert enough force to make a magnetic needle spin in a compass. Stronger electric currents and stronger magnets could be combined to spin a motor. Using Ørsted's discovery, the first electromagnet and the first electric motor were both built by 1823.

The English scientist Michael Faraday made the next major contribution to the understanding of electricity and magnets. Faraday was a brilliant experimenter. He knew from Ørsted's experiment that a moving current could create magnetic force. He wondered if the opposite was also true. Could a magnet cause an electric current to flow in a wire?

Faraday's answer turned out to be one of the most useful discoveries in the history of science. In 1831 Faraday made a circuit with a coil of wire. In the circuit was a galvanometer, which is an instrument that measures small amounts of electric current. Faraday then put a magnet inside the coil of wire. He discovered that a current was created in the wire whenever the magnet was moved in or out of the coil. When the magnet was just sitting still, no electricity flowed. From this experiment came what is known as *Faraday's law:* A moving magnetic field creates an electric current in a wire.

Why was Faraday's discovery so useful? Faraday quickly realized that moving a wire through a powerful magnetic field could generate an electric current. That same year, he built the first electromagnetic generator. Faraday's generator could produce a steady supply of electricity whenever it was needed. Faraday's invention didn't depend on expensive, messy supplies of chemicals as batteries did. And it never ran out of power. Huge modern-day descendants of Faraday's first generator produce the electricity for our TVs, refrigerators, electric lights, and all our many other electrical appliances.

In 1864 James Clerk Maxwell took all the pieces of the electricity and magnetism puzzle and put them together. His mathematical laws of electromagnetism are known as

Maxwell's equations. The mathematical statements of the laws are too complicated to go into here, but his laws tell us the following things:

- Electricity and magnetism are two different aspects of the same force.
- Every electrical charge has an electrical field around it. This field attracts opposite charges and repels like charges.
- A moving electrical charge or field generates a magnetic field.
- A moving magnetic field generates an electrical field.

Since 1864 experiments have shown Maxwell's laws to be correct again and again. Because magnetism and electricity are just different aspects of the same force, scientists usually refer to that force as electromagnetic force. Along with gravitation and the nuclear forces in atoms, it is one of the basic forces of the universe.

As Maxwell considered his discovery, he realized something else that was very interesting. A change in an electric field creates a change in a magnetic field. But a change in a magnetic field then creates a change in an electric field. This process can continue on and on. So a single change in an electric or magnetic field spreads out very rapidly, creating an electromagnetic wave effect.

Maxwell calculated how quickly this electromagnetic wave would move through space. His results said that it would travel at 300,000 kilometers per second (186,000 miles per second). But that is a well-known speed. It is the speed of light. Could it be that light is a form of electromagnetic energy?

Yes. Maxwell discovered that light is an electromagnetic wave. More recent discoveries have shown that light radiation is actually generated by the rapid vibration of electrons in atoms.

Maxwell also predicted that researchers would find other kinds of electromagnetic radiation besides visible light. Maxwell's equations said there should be waves with lower amounts of energy than visible light, and waves with higher amounts of energy.

Two of these other kinds of light waves were already known. Infrared and ultraviolet light had both been discovered around 1800. Maxwell's calculations showed that these light waves are forms of electromagnetic radiation, just as visible light is. And it wasn't long after Maxwell's laws were published that other new forms of electromagnetic radiation were discovered.

In 1889 Heinrich Hertz discovered the existence of radio waves. These are electromagnetic waves with much longer wavelengths than visible light. In 1895 Wilhelm Roentgen discovered X rays. These are electromagnetic waves with very short wavelengths. The wide range of radiation—from radio waves, through infrared waves, visible light, ultraviolet light, and powerful X rays and gamma rays—is known as the electromagnetic spectrum. All these different rays travel at 300,000 kilometers per second. They all behave as visible light does. Maxwell's predictions about electromagnetic energy were proved true!

In 1897 J. J. Thomson discovered the existence of a negatively charged particle smaller than an atom. This particle became known as the electron. Scientists realized that it is the motion of electrons that carries electrical energy.

When a balloon is rubbed against wool, some electrons are transferred from the wool fibers to the rubber. It is that transfer that creates the electrical charge. When we connect a wire to both terminals of a battery, it is the flow of electrons that creates an electric current. And when we turn on a lamp, it is the vibration of electrons in the filament of the lightbulb that creates the electromagnetic waves we call light.

It's hard to imagine what modern-day life would be like

without electric power. Understanding electromagnetic force has made many amazing devices possible. We use this energy to run our appliances, heat and light our homes, and calculate our household budgets. Computers, television, tape recorders, radar, and a thousand other miraculous devices depend on our understanding of electromagnetism.

CHAPTER 3

Electric Current—Ohm's Law and Joule's Law

Electricity has become the most widely used form of energy in our modern world. But to put electricity to use, we must know how it acts in a circuit. With that knowledge, electrical appliances and equipment can be designed to work safely and efficiently.

In the 1800s, electricity was thought of as a flow of electrical charges through any conductor, such as a wire. We now know that those electrical charges are tiny particles called electrons. Electrical energy is actually the movement of electrons in the circuit.

A circuit is the path through which electrical current flows. It is usually a series of wires and electrical devices connected to a source of electrical energy.

The electrical energy in a circuit is generated by a power source. This source can be a battery, which makes electrical energy by chemical reaction. Or it can be a generator, which produces electricity by moving wires through a magnetic field. Commercial power companies generate electricity with huge dynamos powered by water power, coal or oil furnaces, or nuclear reactors.

The power source, either generator or battery, creates an electromotive force. You can think of electromotive force as the amount of electrical "pressure" that sends the current around the circuit. The electromotive force in a circuit is measured in volts (named in honor of Alessandrdo Volta, the inventor of the battery).

The electromotive force is often called a potential difference, or just potential. It produces an electric current only when a circuit connecting the positive and negative poles of the power source is completed. Otherwise, it just has the potential, or possibility, of creating a flow of current. A 6-volt battery has 6 volts of electrical potential whether it is connected to a circuit or not.

The amount of electrical charge flowing through a circuit is called the current. It is measured in amperes (named for André-Marie Ampère, another scientist who worked with electricity). Amperes measure the number of electrons flowing through the circuit per second.

Remember that current and voltage are two different things. It is possible to have a large amount of current flowing through a circuit at a low voltage or a little bit of current flowing at a very high voltage. Voltage measures the electric force, and amperage measures the total amount of electricity that is flowing in a circuit.

As electricity flows around a circuit, it meets with resistance. Resistance is anything that restricts or opposes the flow of electricity in a circuit. Resistance in a circuit turns some of the electrical energy into heat. Electrical resistance is measured in ohms (named for Georg Ohm, about whom we will learn more shortly).

Everything in an electric circuit, including the wires, develops some resistance. The amount of resistance in a circuit depends on four things: the length of the circuit, the thickness of the wires and other conductors in the circuit, the kind of material the wires are made of, and the temperature of the circuit.

Some wires, like those made of silver or copper, have very little resistance. They conduct electricity quite well. Very little of the electrical energy passing through copper wire is turned into heat by resistance. That's why copper is often used for electric circuits. Others have more resistance. For example, Nichrome wire, which is made from a combination of nickel and chromium, has a lot of resistance. It gets very hot when a current passes through it. For this reason, Nichrome is used for the heating elements in toasters and hair dryers.

Some materials, like glass and rubber, have so much resistance that electricity won't flow through them at all. Materials like these are used as insulators.

The longer a piece of wire is, the more resistance it has. And the thicker a wire is, the less resistance it has. Like water flowing through a large pipe, electricity flows more easily through a thick conductor.

The temperature of a material also affects its resistance. In most cases, electrical resistance increases as the temperature increases. But there are exceptions to this rule.

To better understand the movement of electricity in a circuit, picture the similarities between an electric circuit and a system of water pipes. In a water system, the water is forced through the pipes by a pump. The pump corresponds to the generator or battery in an electric circuit. The pump creates pressure, which forces the water through the system. This pressure corresponds to the electromotive force, or voltage. The amount of water flowing through the pipes corresponds to the amount of current flowing through a circuit.

Resistance is similar to the friction (rubbing) in the pipes of a water system. The pump must push against this friction to move the water. When two materials rub

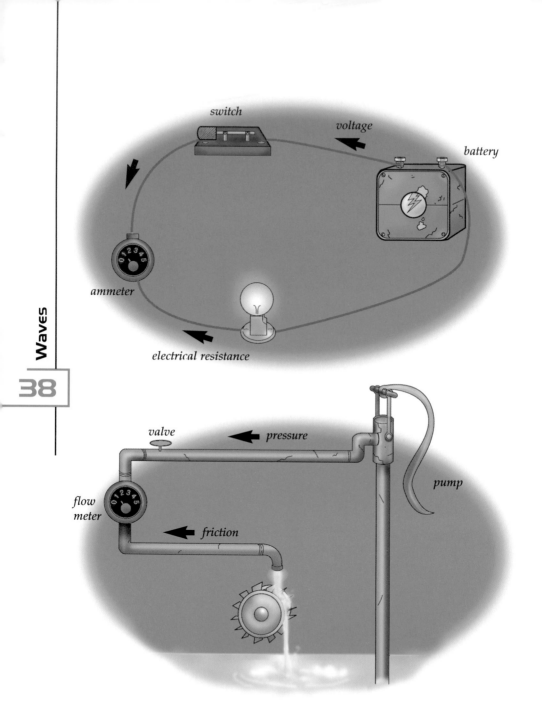

switch

voltage

battery

ammeter

electrical resistance

valve   pressure

flow
meter   pump

friction

An electrical circuit has many similarities to a circular water system.

together, friction generates heat. Like friction, resistance in an electric circuit generates heat. Large pipes allow water to flow more easily, while small pipes have much more friction to restrict the flow. Thicker wires also have less resistance to electrical flow than thin wires.

In the early 1800s, the German physicist Georg Ohm investigated the workings of electric circuits. He wanted to know how resistance and voltage affect the flow of electric current in a wire. Ohm found that when he increased the voltage in a circuit, the amount of current also increased, as long as everything else in the circuit stayed the same. Suppose we had a 10-volt circuit with 1 ampere of current flowing through it. If we doubled the voltage of the circuit to 20 volts, we would also double the amount of current to 2 amps.

Ohm also discovered that the amount of current flowing through a circuit decreased when he increased the amount of resistance in the circuit. If we made the wire in our 10-volt circuit twice as long, that would create twice as much resistance. As a result, only half an ampere of current would flow through the circuit.

In 1827 Ohm published his findings. These discoveries are now known as *Ohm's law.* Ohm's law is stated like this: The flow of current in a circuit is directly proportional to the electromotive force (voltage) and inversely proportional to resistance.

Think about our comparison between electricity and water flow one more time. The amount of water flowing through a pipe depends on the pressure of the water and the size of the pipe. If the pump increases the pressure (higher pressure is like higher voltage), more water will flow through the pipe. If the pipe is made thinner (thinner pipe is like more resistance), less water will flow through it. Ohm's law tells us that something very similar happens with electricity. The amount of electricity flowing in a circuit depends on the voltage (electric "pressure") and the resistance of the circuit.

Mathematically, Ohm's law is written like this:

$$\text{current} = \text{voltage}/\text{resistance} \quad \text{or} \quad I = E/R$$

In this equation, I stands for the intensity, or amount, of current in amperes. E stands for the electromotive force, or voltage, of the circuit. R stands for the resistance.

Notice that the amount of current (I) is expressed as a fraction. If we increase the voltage (E), the numerator of the fraction gets larger. So the value of the fraction as a whole is larger. More voltage in the circuit results in more current.

But when we increase the resistance (R), the denominator of the fraction becomes larger. That makes the value of the fraction smaller. More resistance in the circuit results in less current.

Ohm's law tells us that when there is a lot of resistance, less current will flow. If there is less resistance, more current will flow. That explains why people receive the most dangerous electric shocks when their skin is wet.

Dry skin is not a good conductor. It has lots of resistance. So when a person with dry skin accidentally touches electrical wires and completes a circuit, not much current can flow through the body. That small amount of current does little harm. But if a person is damp, especially if he or she is touching a good conductor like water or metal, the electrical resistance is much less. The person becomes a much better conductor, so more current can flow through the body, causing a dangerous shock.

A few years after Georg Ohm made his discovery, the English physicist James Joule made his own investigation of how electrical energy works. Joule was interested in how one form of energy can be converted to another. One of the changes he studied was the conversion of electric energy to heat.

Power is the amount of energy delivered in each unit of time. Electric power is measured in watts (named in honor of James Watt, inventor of the steam engine). Joule measured the power that electric circuits deliver by seeing how much heat they could generate in a certain amount of time. Much of the electric power in our homes is used the same way—for heat to keep us warm or to cook our food.

Joule found that the amount of power in an electric circuit depends on two things: the voltage of the circuit and the amount of current flowing in it. The more current a circuit has, the more power it delivers. And the more voltage a circuit has, the more power it delivers. The power produced by a circuit can be calculated by multiplying the voltage times the amount of current:

$$\text{power} = \text{voltage} \times \text{current} \quad \text{or} \quad H = E \times I$$

This rule is known as *Joule's law.* Joule's law tells us that increasing either the current or the voltage in a circuit increases the power that the circuit produces.

All the electrical appliances we plug into our household circuits use electrical energy to do work. They transform the electrical energy into heat, light, or motion. The appliances all add more resistance in the circuits. It is the resistance in the wires of an oven that generates the heat to bake our bread or roast our chicken for dinner. This intentional resistance in a circuit is called the load.

The electric motors in our blenders, washing machines, and vacuum cleaners all have electrical resistance. They place an increased load on the circuit as they are running. If you place your hand near the electric motor of any appliance, you will be able to feel the heat that its electrical resistance generates.

In ordinary house current, the voltage always stays about the same—110 or 220 volts. But the electric company will supply a household with as much current as it can use. So when we need more power to run our home appliances, the amount of current in the circuits increases. In our homes, when we use more power, we have more amperes flowing through our circuits.

Joule's law explains why an electric oven is more expensive to use than a toaster. An electric oven needs to produce much more heat than a little toaster does. So ovens use a lot more current than toasters. More current flowing through an appliance generates more power, or more heat. But we have to buy that power from the electric company. The more power we use, the more we have to pay.

Joule's law also explains why we put fuses or circuit breakers in the electric circuits in our homes. When we overload a circuit with too many appliances, the wires must carry a large amount of current. Wires all have some resistance to the flow of electricity, and resistance generates heat. The more current that is flowing in the wires, the more heat that is produced. If the wires get too hot, they can easily start a fire.

A "short circuit" occurs when the two wires in a circuit touch without an appliance in the circuit. That can happen if the insulation on the wires melts or gets worn. Without the resistance of an appliance in the circuit, a large amount of current will flow easily through the wires. All that current can also create enough heat in the wires to start a fire.

Fortunately, every household circuit also has a fuse or circuit breaker in it. Fuses act just like any other piece of wire in a circuit. They conduct electricity as part of the circuit, and they also have some resistance. They get hotter and hotter as more current flows through them. But fuses are designed to melt when too much current passes through them. When a fuse melts, it breaks the electric circuit. No more current can flow. That puts an end to the electrical overload that might otherwise get hot enough to cause a fire. Circuit breakers perform the same safety function, but they don't have to be replaced each time they "blow."

Every time you turn on a light or make a piece of toast or iron a shirt, the discoveries of Georg Ohm, James Joule, and their fellow researchers are working for you. Understanding Ohm's law, Joule's law, and the other laws of circuits allows electricians and electrical engineers to make our electrified world safe and efficient.

Scientists now understand the workings of electrical current very well. But there is still much more to learn about our universe. We still have much to learn about the stars and planets, the atom, and the miracles of life. There are still more laws to discover and more mysteries to solve. Perhaps you may one day add your name to that distinguished list of scientists who have helped discover the secrets of the universe.

Inverse Square Laws

A number of important natural laws all follow a similar pattern. This pattern is known as an inverse square law. Gravitational force behaves in this way. So do electrical and magnetic forces. So does the intensity of light. It isn't an accident that all these laws are so similar. Here is an explanation of why inverse square laws apply to so many different kinds of forces.

In all inverse square laws, the strength of the force that the law describes is inversely proportional to the distance from the source of the force. When two quantities are inversely proportional, one measurement decreases as the other one increases. The intensity of a force decreases as the distance increases. In all inverse square laws, however, the intensity decreases in proportion to the square of the distance from the center of force.

The intensity of light follows an inverse square law. The intensity of light is inversely proportional to the square of the distance from the light source. As you get farther from a light source, the brightness of the light from that source decreases. Let's use light as an example to see why so many different forces follow this one pattern.

Imagine a source of light such as a tiny electric bulb in the middle of a large, dark space. The light spreads out from the source in all directions, like an expanding bubble. Light intensity is measured in lumens. Let's suppose our light source is producing a total of 1,000 lumens of light.

Picture a sphere with a 1-meter (about 3 feet) radius surrounding the light source. The light from the source illuminates the inside of the sphere. How much area does the light have to illuminate? The surface area of a sphere is calculated by multiplying 4 times π (pi, or 3.14) times the square of the radius of the sphere.

$$A = 4 \times \pi \times r^2$$

So our sphere has a surface area of 12.6 square meters (136 square feet). The 1,000 lumens of light produced by the bulb will be distributed evenly around those 12.6 square meters of surface.

Dividing the total amount of light by the number of square meters in the sphere will tell us how much light is shining on each square meter. When we divide 1,000 lumens among 12.6 square meters, we find that each square meter is illuminated with about 80 lumens of light.

Suppose we double the radius of the sphere surrounding our light source. You will see that the 1,000 lumens of light get distributed over a much larger area. The new sphere has a radius of 2 meters (about 6 feet). To compute the total surface area, again we multiply $4 \times \pi \times r^2$. Our new sphere has an area of 50.2 square meters (540 square feet). The radius of the new sphere is only twice the radius of the first sphere. But the area of the second sphere is four times the area of the first. That is because the area of a sphere is based on the square of the radius.

Our light source is still producing the same amount of light: 1,000 lumens. But at this distance, that same amount of light is shining on a sphere with 50.2 square meters of area. So each square meter receives only about 20 lumens of light. This is only one-fourth of the amount of light that each square meter received in the first sphere. The distance from the light source to the sphere has doubled, but the intensity of the light is only one-fourth as great. This is an inverse square relationship.

The same thing holds true if the radius is increased to 3 meters (about 10 feet). Once again we multiply $4 \times \pi \times r^2$. Our third sphere has a surface area of 113 square meters (1,216 square feet). The radius of this sphere is three times as big as the radius of the original sphere, but the area of the third sphere is nine times larger. Our 1,000 lumens of light are spread out across 113 square meters of area. Each square meter of our third sphere receives about 9 lumens of light.

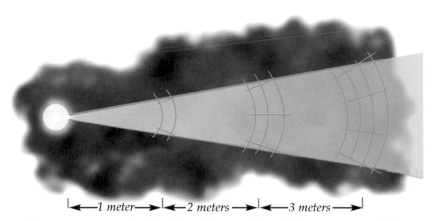

|←——1 meter——→|←—2 meters —→|←—3 meters —→|

The same amount of light, as it spreads out from a source, fills an increasingly large area.

This is only one-ninth of the amount each square meter received in the first sphere. The distance from the center to the sphere has now tripled, but the intensity of the light is only one-ninth as great.

Of course, the spheres don't actually exist. The imaginary spheres simply give us a way of picturing why the intensity of the light decreases much more quickly than the distance increases. It's because the total amount of energy gets spread out over a rapidly expanding area.

You should even be able to see this inverse square law happening with your own eyes. Mark off distances of 10, 20, and 30 meters (30, 60, 90 feet) from a 0 point in your backyard or on the sidewalk near your house. When it gets dark, stand on your 0 point. Ask someone to stand with a flashlight on the 10-meter mark. Look at the intensity of the light. Have the person move to the 20-meter mark and then the 30-meter mark, and compare what you see. Although you won't be able to measure the intensity unless you have a very sensitive light meter, you should be able to tell that it is decreasing rapidly as your assistant moves farther away.

You can picture gravitational force spreading out from the center of the Earth (or any other mass) in the same way

that light spreads out from a light source. You can picture
an electromagnetic field spreading outward from a source
in a similar way. Picture each force spreading outward from
its source like an ever-expanding bubble. Inverse square
relationships hold true for all these forces because they all
spread out evenly in all directions from the center point at
which they are generated. As you get farther and farther
away from the center point, the effect of these forces is
spread over a much larger area.

Waves

48

1620	The *Mayflower* lands in Massachusetts
1633	Galileo is convicted of heresy by the Inquisition and placed under house arrest
1668	Isaac Newton makes the first reflecting telescope
1678	**Christiaan Huygens proposes his wave theory of light**
1687	Isaac Newton publishes his *Principia*
1692	Witchcraft trials take place in Salem, Massachusetts
1704	**Isaac Newton publishes *Opticks*, including his particle theory of light**
1732	Benjamin Franklin begins publishing *Poor Richard's Almanack*
1752	Benjamin Franklin discovers the electrical nature of lightning through his kite-flying experiment
1775–1783	American War of Independence
1776	American Declaration of Independence is written
1789	George Washington becomes the first president of the United States
1800	**William Herschel discovers infrared radiation; Alessandro Volta introduces his electric cell (battery)**
1801	Johann Ritter discovers ultraviolet radiation
1801–1804	**Thomas Young studies light and discovers that it creates interference patterns**

1820	**Hans Christian Ørsted discovers that an electric current creates a magnetic field**
1827	**Georg Ohm publishes his law on the relationship of electric current, voltage, and resistance**
1829	Louis Braille's system of writing for the blind is first published (revised in 1837)
1831	**Michael Faraday discovers that a moving magnetic field produces an electric current**
1834	Charles Wheatstone measures the speed of electric current in a wire
1849	**Armand Fizeau measures the speed of light**
1859	Charles Darwin publishes *On the Origin of Species by Means of Natural Selection*
1861–1865	American Civil War
1864	**Maxwell's equations on magnetism and electricity are published**
1865	President Abraham Lincoln is assassinated
1876	Alexander Graham Bell patents the telephone
1882	Thomas Edison's generating station in New York begins providing electricity to individual consumers
1886–1889	**Heinrich Hertz discovers radio waves**
1895	**Wilhelm Roentgen discovers X rays**
1897	**J. J. Thomson discovers the electron**
1905	Albert Einstein publishes his special theory of relativity, including $E=mc^2$
1914–1918	World War I
1922	British Broadcasting Company (BBC) makes the first public radio broadcast
1939–1945	World War II

49

Timeline

André-Marie Ampère (1775–1836) was a French physicist who showed a great talent for mathematics very early in his life. His photographic memory, combined with a love of reading, allowed him to study many subjects on his own. Ampère founded the field of electromagnetism and was the first scientist to develop a method for measuring electricity. Despite his outstanding career, his personal life was often troubled. His father was guillotined when Ampère was only eighteen, his first wife died very young, and his second marriage was unsuccessful.

Charles-Augustin de Coulomb (1736–1806) was a French scientist who worked as a military engineer for most of his career. While in the army, he spent nine years on the tropical West Indies island of Martinique, where he helped rebuild destroyed forts. Back home in France, he continued to work for the military but also began studying physics. He is best known for his contributions to the study of magnetic and electrical forces.

Albert Einstein (1879–1955) was born in Germany. He was a student who enjoyed reading but disliked lectures and tests, so he was never a particular favorite with his teachers. His undistinguished university record led him to a job as a clerk in a Swiss patent office. From these modest beginnings, he went on to introduce the theory of relativity, which changed the world of physics forever. Einstein was named a public enemy by the Nazis in Germany. He acted as an unofficial adviser to President Franklin D. Roosevelt on the threat of the atomic bomb. He was even offered the presidency of Israel. In his private life, however, he had simple, quiet tastes. His hobbies included music and sailing.

Michael Faraday (1791–1867) was a British chemist and physicist who discovered his love of science by chance. Working as a bookbinder to help support his father, a blacksmith in poor health, Faraday often read the books he bound. He came upon several that dealt with physics and chemistry. These encounters led to the beginning of a great career, during which he discovered the laws of electrolysis, invented an electric motor and generator, and formulated his law on electromagnetic fields.

Armand Fizeau (1819–1896) was a French physicist with a particular interest in optics. He studied the emerging science of photography and in 1845 played a role in taking the first detailed pictures of the Sun. He also studied the way light passes through water, both still and moving. One of his most significant accomplishments was measuring the speed of light.

Benjamin Franklin (1706–1790) was an American politician and author. He did not begin scientific work until he was forty years old, yet he made some of the greatest advances of his time in the study of electricity. The phenomenon of electricity was very fashionable in the mid-1700s, but Franklin took the matter more seriously and conducted many experiments. His theory of negative and positive electrical charges and his law of conservation of charge were important contributions.

Galileo Galilei (1564–1642) was born in Pisa, Italy. He was one of the first scientists to regard experimentation and mathematics as necessary companions to observation. Using these tools, he made great discoveries, often contradicting long-accepted beliefs and bringing him into conflict with other scientists and with the Catholic Church. He made important but controversial strides with his inclined-plane experiments, which disproved Aristotle's theory that heavy objects fall faster than light ones. A more dramatic conflict was caused by his support of Copernicus's heliocentric (Sun-centered) model of the solar system. For this, Galileo was tried by the Inquisition in 1633 and sentenced by the Church to house arrest.

William Herschel (1738–1822) was born in Germany but settled in England when he was nineteen years old. Though he was to make his name as an astronomer, his first jobs were as a musician. While working as an organist in Bath, England, his hobby was making and using telescopes. He discovered the planet Uranus in 1781, after which he was appointed the Court Astronomer to King George III. Herschel cataloged hundreds of stars, identified the Milky Way as a galaxy, and discovered infrared light.

Heinrich Hertz (1857–1894) was a German physicist. He was a talented student whose many strengths included fluency in several languages. In college he originally studied engineering, but his true love was physics. He became a pupil of Hermann von Helmholtz in Berlin. At Helmholtz's urging, he focused his attention on electromagnetic radiation. One of the most significant results of his work was the discovery of radio waves.

Robert Hooke (1635–1703) was a British scientist who planned to enter the church as a profession but whose health was considered too fragile for the job. Though primarily remembered as a physicist for such work as his law of elasticity and his studies of gravity and light, Hooke successfully tried his hand at many areas of science. A talented mechanic, he developed or improved the compound microscope, the barometer, and a telegraph system. He also studied chemistry, particularly combustion, and even ventured into biology—Hooke was the first to use the term "cell" in a biological context.

Christiaan Huygens (1629–1695) was born to a wealthy Dutch family in The Hague. Educated in science and mathematics, he was one of many physicists to be puzzled and intrigued by the nature of light. In 1678 Huygens proposed his wave theory of light, which was contrary to the particle theory supported by Newton; not until well after both their deaths would the dual nature of light be discovered. Another of his great contributions to physics was his study of the pendulum and its applications to timekeeping and clocks. Huygens also had an interest in astronomy; he discovered both the rings and the largest moon of Saturn, and he had many theories regarding extraterrestrial life.

James Prescott Joule (1818–1889) was a British physicist. He was the son of a brewer in Manchester, England. Shy and rather sickly as a child, he was educated at home by tutors. His science and math teacher was the eminent physicist John Dalton. Joule was particularly interested in the study of electricity and heat, and he conducted many imaginative and careful experiments. His work led to the formulation of Joule's law on current and resistance. He was also a contributor to the law of conservation of energy.

James Clerk Maxwell (1831–1879) was a Scottish physicist who was educated in Edinburgh, Scotland, and Cambridge, England. Though teased as a child and rather shy and eccentric as an adult, he became one of the most prominent names in science. He is known largely for his findings on electromagnetism

(Maxwell's equations) and for his contribution to the kinetic theory of gases. Maxwell also studied such varied subjects as color blindness, photography, and the rings of Saturn.

Albert Michelson (1852–1931) was born in Prussia (modern-day northern Germany and northern Poland), but his family immigrated to the United States when Michelson was four years old. He attended the Naval Academy in Annapolis, Maryland. As an officer, he taught physics and chemistry. When his duties required him to teach his students how to measure the speed of light, he dedicated himself to finding more accurate ways to do so. After leaving the navy, he became a physics professor. His many optical experiments, some conducted in cooperation with Edward Morley, helped lead to the development of Einstein's theory of relativity. In 1907 Michelson became the first American to receive the Nobel Prize in physics.

Isaac Newton (1642–1727) was born in Lincolnshire, England. An unconventional student who didn't care much how he looked, Newton was a brilliant mathematician and scientist. Just a few of Newton's many important contributions to science include the law of universal gravitation, the three laws of motion, the basic elements of calculus, and the particle theory of light. Newton also served as the Warden and later the Master of the Mint. In 1705 he was knighted, partly for his work reforming the British currency. Late in his life, Newton worked less on scientific and mathematical matters, turning instead to the study of alchemy, theology, and history.

Georg Ohm (1789–1854) was born in Erlangen, Bavaria (modern-day Germany), and studied science and mathematics at the University of Erlangen. Ohm dreamed of becoming a prominent professor at a major German university, but he worked for many years as a relatively low-ranking instructor at various schools. His most famous discovery, Ohm's law, states that electrical current is directly proportional to voltage and inversely proportional to resistance. Because Ohm's income was small, this important discovery was made using fairly simple instruments and homemade metal wire! Ohm also studied the way that the human ear processes sound waves. In 1849 he finally became a professor of physics in Munich.

Hans Christian Ørsted (1777–1851) was a Danish physicist. After studying pharmacy and physical science at the University of Copenhagen, he did not immediately settle down to a research career. First he spent several years traveling, during which he wrote and gave lectures. Ørsted's most famous discovery, that an electric current creates a magnetic field, laid the foundation for the study of electromagnetism.

Max Planck (1858–1947) was a German physicist. A brilliant student in many areas, including music, Planck became especially interested in the study of light. His investigations of light waves led to his discovery of quanta, the individual packets of energy that make up light. This discovery was revolutionary, winning him the Nobel Prize and defining the break between classical and modern physics. In contrast to his great professional success, Planck had a tragic personal life. His wife died after twenty-two years of marriage, one son was killed in World War I, his twin daughters both died in childbirth, and his other son was executed during World War II.

Wilhelm Roentgen (1845–1923) was a German physicist who originally intended to be an engineer. While studying in Zurich, Switzerland, he became more interested in physics and graduated in that field instead. In 1895 Roentgen conducted experiments with electrical current that eventually led to his discovery of mysterious invisible rays that he named X rays. Roentgen found that these X rays easily passed through some substances, such as wood and paper. Other materials, such as bone and metal, stopped the rays. In 1901 he was awarded the first Nobel Prize in physics for his discovery.

Olaus Rømer (1644–1710) was a Danish astronomer. He made his name by determining that light has a finite (limited) speed. Many contemporary scientists had begun to believe that light was not capable of infinite velocity, as was previously thought. While working at the Paris Observatory in France, Rømer became the first to prove the theory through his observations of the eclipses of Jupiter's moons. He measured the speed of light to be about 150,000 miles per second, which was remarkably accurate for that time. He later moved back to Denmark and in 1705 became the mayor of Copenhagen.

Joseph John (J. J.) Thomson (1856–1940) was a British physicist who originally intended to be an engineer. When his father died in 1872, Thomson could not afford the fee to become an apprentice and turned instead to mathematics and physics. After graduating from Trinity College in Cambridge, he became a professor there. He did extensive work in electromagnetism, leading to his revolutionary discovery of the electron. Thomson's work led, in turn, to Rutherford's discovery of the proton and the beginnings of nuclear physics. Thomson enjoyed many recreations. He was a great fan of cricket and rugby, and he especially loved plants and gardening.

Alessandro Volta (1745–1827) was an Italian physicist who, in his youth, seemed more interested in the arts than in science. He wrote sonnets in Italian and French and odes in Latin. At the age of nineteen, Volta became interested in science, particularly electricity. He conducted many experiments using electricity and invented several devices to produce and measure electrostatic charge. His most famous invention, however, was the battery, which produced the world's first continuous electric current. Even Napoleon was impressed. In 1801 he named Volta a count of the kingdom of Lombardy (modern-day Italy).

James Watt (1736–1819) was a Scottish engineer. He was a sickly child whose education was frequently interrupted by illness. Still, he managed to become an instrument maker. While working in Glasgow, he was asked to repair a Newcomen steam engine, the most advanced model at that time. After studying the machine, Watt was convinced that he could find a more efficient design. He formed a partnership with a manufacturer, and several years later they produced a greatly improved steam engine that played an important part in the industrial revolution. Its wide use in factories allowed him to retire as a wealthy man in 1800.

Thomas Young (1773–1829) was a British scientist whose talents were incredibly diverse. He showed his brilliance early, learning to read at the age of two. By age fourteen, he had studied thirteen languages and written an autobiography in Latin. Young's family encouraged him to become a doctor. As a medical student, he studied the eye and the mechanics of vision. These interests led to his study of optics. He proved that light both diffracts and produces interference patterns. These findings contributed to the particle/wave debate surrounding the nature of light. In 1814, when the Rosetta Stone was brought to London from Egypt, Young studied the stone along with other scholars. He played an important role in breaking the code of hieroglyphics.

For Further Reading

Asimov, Isaac. *Asimov's Chronology of Science and Discovery.* New York: HarperCollins, 1994.

Cobb, Vicki, and Josh Cobb. *Light Action! Amazing Experiments with Optics.* New York: HarperCollins, 1993.

Friedhoffer, Robert. *Physics Lab in the Home.* New York: Franklin Watts, 1997.

Gardner, Robert. *Optics.* New York: Twenty-First Century Books, 1994.

_____. *Science Projects about Electricity and Magnets.* Springfield, NJ: Enslow Publishers, 1994.

Henderson, Harry, and Lisa Yount. *The Scientific Revolution.* San Diego: Lucent Books, 1996.

Lloyd, Gill, and David Jefferis. *The History of Optics.* New York: Thomson Learning, 1995.

Meadows, Jack. *The Great Scientists.* New York: Oxford University Press, 1997.

Parker, Steve. *Electricity.* New York: Dorling Kindersley, 1992.

Skurzynski, Gloria. *Waves: The Electromagnetic Universe.* Washington, D.C.: The National Geographic Society, 1996.

Spangenburg, Ray. *The History of Science from the Ancient Greeks to the Scientific Revolution.* New York: Facts on File, 1993.

Wilkinson, Philip, and Michael Pollard. *Scientists Who Changed the World.* New York: Chelsea House Publishers, 1994.

Wood, Robert W. *Who?: Famous Experiments for the Young Scientist.* Philadelphia: Chelsea House Publishers, 1999.

Websites

BBC Online's science site
<http://www.bbc.co.uk/science>

Boston Museum of Science online exhibits
Includes a Theater of Electricity exhibit.
<http://www.mos.org/exhibits/online_exhibits.html>

Center for History of Physics, sponsored by the American Institute of Physics
<http://www.aip.org/history/index.html>

Cool Science, sponsored by the U.S. Department of Energy
<http://www.fetc.doe.gov/coolscience/index.html>

Kid's Castle, sponsored by the Smithsonian Institution
Includes a science site.
<http://www.kidscastle.si.edu/>

NPR's *Sounds Like Science* site
<http://www.npr.org/programs/science>

PBS's *A Science Odyssey* site
<http://www.pbs.org/wgbh/aso>

San Francisco's Exploratorium
<http://www.exploratorium.edu/>

Science Museum of Minnesota
<http://www.smm.org>

For Further Reading

Adler, Irving. *The Wonders of Physics: An Introduction to the Physical World.* New York: Golden Press, 1966.

Asimov, Isaac. *Asimov's New Guide to Science.* New York: Basic Books, 1984.

Freeman, Ira M. *Light and Radiation.* New York: Random House, 1965.

Gamow, George. *Biography of Physics.* New York: Harper & Row, 1961.

Goldstein-Jackson, Kevin. *Experiments with Everyday Objects: Science Activities for Children, Parents and Teachers.* Englewood Cliffs, NJ: Prentice-Hall, 1978.

Kent, Amanda, and Alan Ward. *Introduction to Physics.* Tulsa, OK: Usborne Publishing Ltd., 1983.

Math, Irwin. *Wires and Watts: Understanding and Using Electricity.* New York: Charles Scribner's Sons, 1981.

Millar, David, Ian Millar, John Millar, and Margaret Millar. *The Cambridge Dictionary of Scientists.* New York: Cambridge University Press, 1996.

Ruchlis, Hy. *Bathtub Physics.* New York: Harcourt, Brace and World, 1967.

Sagan, Carl. *Cosmos.* New York: Random House, 1980.

Sullivan, Walter. *Black Holes.* New York: Anchor/Doubleday, 1979.

Von Baeyer, Hans C. *Rainbows, Snowflakes and Quarks: Physics and the World Around Us.* New York: McGraw-Hill, 1984.

Weart, Spencer R. *Light: A Key to the Universe.* New York: Coward-McCann, 1973.

Wilson, Mitchell. *Seesaws to Cosmic Rays: A First View of Physics.* New York: Lothrop, Lee & Shepard, 1967.

conservation of charge, law of: for every negative charge created, there must be an equal amount of positive charge

Coulomb's law: the electrical force between two objects is directly proportional to the amount of charge in the two objects and inversely proportional to the square of their distance

current: the rate of flow of electric charge, measured in amperes

diffraction: the curving of a wave around an obstacle

electromagnetic spectrum: the entire range of electromagnetic radiation, including radio waves, infrared waves, visible light, ultraviolet light, X rays, and gamma rays

electromotive force: the electrical force sending current around a circuit, measured in volts. Also called potential difference.

Faraday's law: a moving magnetic field creates an electric current in a wire

Huygens' principle: each point along a wave acts as a source of new waves with the same characteristics as the original wave

Joule's law: increasing either the current or the voltage in a circuit increases the power that the circuit produces

Maxwell's equations: a set of mathematical laws describing electricity and magnetism

Ohm's law: the current in a circuit is directly proportional to the electromotive force and inversely proportional to the resistance

power: the rate at which energy is delivered, measured in watts

reflection, law of: the angle at which a wave hits a surface is equal to the angle at which it is reflected from the surface

refraction: the bending of a wave at the boundary between two materials

resistance: anything that restricts or opposes the flow of electricity in a circuit, measured in ohms

About the Author

Paul Fleisher has written more than twenty books for young people and educators, including *Life Cycles of a Dozen Diverse Creatures*, the *Webs of Life* series, and *Brain Food*. His most recent books are *Gorillas* and *Ice Cream Treats: The Inside Scoop*. Paul is a regular contributor to *Technology and Learning* magazine. He has also created several pieces of educational software, including the award-winning *Perplexing Puzzles*.

Paul has taught in Programs for the Gifted in Richmond, Virginia, since 1978. He is also active in civic organizations that work for peace and social justice. In 1988 he received the Virginia Education Association's Award for Peace and International Relations, and in 1999 he was awarded the Thomas Jefferson Medal for Outstanding Contributions to Natural Science Education. In his spare time, you may find Paul walking through the woods, gardening, or fishing on the Chesapeake Bay. Paul and his wife, Debra Sims Fleisher, live in Richmond, Virginia.